Moments with God's Word

By

Mary L. Ball

Life Inspiring Books

All scriptures references are from the King James Version of the Bible

Letter from the Author

I am a Christian fiction author. Like many other believers, I sometimes get bogged down; needing to seek solace in God's word. Jesus endured much for us, so we are sure to face adversity in this world.

God's Holy word is full of helpful scriptures. Some are more popular than others. For example the verse in John 3:16 is quoted all across America.

"For God so loved the world, that he gave his only begotten Son, that whosoever believeth in him should not perish, but have everlasting life."

Also, the scripture in Matthew 7:12. We always think of this verse when we notice someone who is not treating others fairly, as the scriptures teach.

"Therefore all things whatsoever ye would that men should do to you, do ye even so to them: for this is the law and the prophets."

The good books in the Bible are full of way-making truths. Some of the verses may stand out more, but every word in the Bible is more precious than gold. Unlike the yellow metal that the world treasures God's Holy word is forevermore, leading us to eternity.

In Moments with God's Word, I want to highlight a few verses that are precious to me and offer magnificent meanings that can have a life-changing effect.

So many wonderful verses in the Bible have illuminated into my life at just the right time.

God's enlighten words are a continued life force for all of us. Be encouraged, with faith. A restful mind is only a knee away.

TABLE OF CONTENTS

CHAPTER ONE

A Look at the Scripture from 1 Peter 5:7

1 Peter 5:7 – "Casting all your care upon him; for he careth for you."

The verse from the book of First Peter is one that many Christians quote. We do our best to live and learn from the truthful writings inspired by God and the words spoken by Jesus Christ.

The cares of life, our families and financial situations will test us to the point of forgetting how steadfast and comforting God's instructions are. Struggles we go though in this world often cause us to forget that the Lord will guide us in all things, if we give him the opportunity.

The Holy Word is immersed with insights handed down to us from the disciples. It offers a wealth of knowledge for us to feed on. We only need to take the time to study and increase our knowledge. In many cases, the understanding of the Bible will not detours us from our purpose of getting closer to Jesus Christ, but the lack of soaking in the richness of his scriptures will cause us to stumble. It is easy to learn a Bible verse and not comprehend how deep those words go. The Lord is Almighty and realizes that as humans we sometimes miss the mark and overlook the importance of a verse. That is why He is always ready to quicken our spirit and teach us insights along the way. I am thankful for the long-suffering He has for humanity.

2 Timothy 2:15 "Study to shew thyself approved unto God, a workman that needeth not to be ashamed, rightly dividing the word of truth."

God's Holy Scriptures gives us a chance to understand that we are not immune from unfailing. We make mistakes just as the disciples did. Still, we must strive to be the best possible witness we can be for God's kingdom and to learn as the Lord instructs. That gives us a chance to help someone else, thus doing God's will.

Romans 3:23 "For all have sinned, and come short of the glory of God;"

We grow each day by drawing on the fruits of the spirit. This message helps to keep us walking in the light. The Holy Spirit imparts inside us the ability to react to the world through using the good fruits. When we, as believers meet with an unkind situation it is imperative that we step back from the circumstance and remember what Jesus expects from us. It can also turn an unfortunate instance into a pleasant experience.

Galatians 5:22-23 "But the fruit of the Spirit is love, joy, peace, longsuffering, gentleness, goodness, faith, 23-Meekness, temperance: against such there is no law."

Peter, an apostle of Jesus fell short. Like every human being, he had many things to learn during his walk. Peter was a fisherman. Jesus saw he would make mistakes but Christ also knew that Peter would go forth and be a worthy servant.

Matthew 4: 18 "And Jesus, walking by the sea of Galilee, saw two brethren, Simon called Peter, and Andrew his brother, casting a net into the sea: for they were fishers."

Indeed Peter did fumble along the way. One of his shortcomings was impulsiveness. Peter asked Jesus to let him walk on the water. After Jesus bid him to come, he took his eyes off the Lord and put them on the turbulent sea. Jesus in his mercy protected Peter.

Matthew 14:29-30 "And he said, Come. And when Peter was come down out of the ship, he walked on the water, to go to Jesus. But when he saw the wind boisterous, he was afraid; and beginning to sink, he cried, saying, Lord, save me."

The Apostle also criticized Jesus when he spoke of his death.

"Matthew 16:22 "Then Peter took him, and began to rebuke him, saying, Be it far from thee, Lord: this shall not be unto thee."

The most famous thing Peter did was in Matthew 26:3 where he assured Jesus he would never deny him, only to speak out three times that he knew not the Lord. These are a few of the things Peter repented from. Jesus knew all this about Peter, just as he knows our weaknesses. The Lord forgave Peter, just as he does us and remains a loving savior.

After Peter endured trials, we learn that in the book of Acts 2:14 he went and spoke to the crowd in Jerusalem. Later, he healed a lame beggar and continued to do marvelous things for the kingdom of God.

Matthew 16:18-19 "And I say also unto thee, That thou art Peter, and upon this rock I will build my church; and the gates of hell shall not prevail against it. And I will give unto thee the keys of the kingdom of heaven: and whatsoever thou shalt bind on earth shall be bound in heaven: and whatsoever thou shalt loose on earth shall be loosed in heaven."

Through all of Peter's missteps, he was a restored worker for God, and preached about our risen Lord. Is it any wonder that Peter stood adamant on the fact that we can cast our cares to the Lord? Peter had some growing pains along the way but he certainly grew into the knowledge of casting and became the rock that Jesus intended for him to be. Now he tells us to give our problems to the Lord.

CHAPTER TWO

What Does It Mean To Cast our Cares?

To a Christian the books in the Holy Bible are a valuable tool that we need for everyday use. They are as important as the light switches in our house.

Without some type of toggle to make a connection from the switch to the wires connected throughout the walls our rooms would stay dark. Thankfully, all we have to do is flip a lever or push the switch and we have light to see by, so we do not stumble.

God's holy word is like that light control. Without the Bible, our lives would be dark and void. We would stagger through life not having any assurance of peace and eternity. It would surely be a bleak existence with no hope. God's word is as true for today as it was several thousand years ago. His scriptures are the most important ingredient in the process of casting our cares. Studying the Bible reinforces God's promises so that when we do cast our troubles we have confidence in the Lord and in His assurances.

The Holy Bible is translated into English for our comprehension. The Old Testament is interpreted from the original Hebrew language. The New Testament, deciphered from Greek. Many of the scriptures we are familiar with have much deeper meanings than we consider. Still, Jesus makes a way for us to understand his teachings.

In 1Peter 5:7 it says, "Casting all your care upon him; for he careth for you."

Care is written in this verse two times. The first word has a different meaning than the last one. Still each term stands strong to help us realize the importance of letting the Lord take over our problems.

Casting all our care. This form of the word "care" used in Peter's verse is translated from the Greek and derives from a root word for, a division or part of. It implies stress. It includes our thoughts, worries or the way we concentrate on worldly concerns to the point of burdening our mind. Peter is showing that this type of care will divide our focus and draw it away from the Lord and His grace. The enemy uses this to distract us in the hope that we will forget who our burden bearer truly is. When we neglect to count on God during the hard times we place a barrier in front of us and make it difficult for God to work.

Matthew 11:28 "Come unto me, all [ye] that labour and are heavy laden, and I will give you rest."

The reference from this word written in Matthew 13:22 further signify the importance of understanding how discord from our lives play havoc and cause a stumbling block.

Matthew 13:22 "He also that received seed among the thorns is he that heareth the word; and the care of this world, and the deceitfulness of riches, choke the word, and he becometh unfruitful."

Notice Jesus is speaking about the parable of the sower. The thorns are ungodly situations. Many trials that we might encounter can try to turn us away from God's word, causing us not to receive all of his promises. Cares not surrendered to the Lord completely can even result in us losing sight of our relationship with God.

1Peter 5:7 "Casting all your care upon him; for he careth for you."

"For he careth." And he really does. One of the many wonderful characteristics of our marvelous Lord. He notices our hardships, no matter who we are. No one is an afterthought for our Heavenly Father. He is always watching over his children.

Matthew 6:25-26 "Therefore I say unto you, Take no thought for your life, what ye shall eat, or what ye shall drink; nor yet for your body, what ye shall put on. Is not the life more than meat, and the body than raiment? Behold the fowls of the air: for they sow not, neither do they reap, nor gather into barns; yet your heavenly Father feedeth them. Are ye not much better than they?"

Even if we stepped out of his grace for a time, a remorseful soul and a humble cry to Jesus Christ will draw us into his arms and bring his unending grace back to us. Anyone who has read the Psalms of David knows how merciful the Lord can be, even when we do make a mistake.

Psalm 40:17 "But I am poor and needy; yet the Lord thinketh upon me: thou art my help and my deliverer; make no tarrying, O my God."

In the challenges from a heavy burden, we must toss or turn over the weight of our concern to Christ. Sometimes our problems will seem huge, but God is above any difficult situation that we encounter. Often times, our grievances can distract us and get our minds off the fact that we must make it a point to cast our burdens to the Lord. Those moments are especially important to gather our fortitude, reaffirm our belief and trust the Lord and all his abilities. That is the strong hold that we have.

Psalm 68:19 "Blessed be the Lord, who daily loadeth us with benefits, even the God of our salvation. Selah."

To cast our burden we must remember that as Christians we belong to God. By faith in Christ, we commit to His calling. When heartache bears on us, it is normal to want to fix our problems. We tend to analyze every situation, and ponder over the outcome. But God's ways are not like ours. He is the Almighty. The Lord sees the big picture, which surrounds our circumstances.

As we study the scriptures, we find countless stories of conquests that only came about because of God's mighty hand.

Victories that seemed impossible.

Daniel, in the lion's den is just one occasion that seemed doomed, but with God, it was possible. We still have the same Lord working for us today, just as he did back then.

Psalms 50:15 "And call upon me in the day of trouble: I will deliver thee, and thou shalt glorify me."

God knows what is best for each of us. He is a deliverer. If we are faced with circumstances, a situation that we believe God hasn't took over yet; it can still feel like a burden. Do not get discouraged; continue to trust that the Lord wants to bless. Even when we find an occasion that is hard to understand or comprehend. God is there, ready to provide us with the knowledge we need. It will come through the wisdom, which is in Christ. Pray for understanding and continue to meditate on His words. More insight from his merciful grace will come.

Put faith in him. Praise him and believe he is the way, the truth and the life. (John 14:6) Take confidence in the fact that Jesus still bears all of our infirmities.

Stand tall and walk in the sometimes-lowly valley. God's promises are for real. Going through trials produces a priority list where worshipping Jesus Christ should be first. Honor the fact that God is sovereign. Study his words; delight in His glory and promises. Turn to God through Jesus Christ, with all requests and leave it in his capable arms.

No more examining problems or exploring solutions.

Lay it all at the foot of the cross and walk away with the assurance that the Lord has it under control.

How can we achieve this?

Thankfully, there are a few different responses to that question.

The main key is to center the attention on Jesus Christ. Be grateful for the gift of salvation He granted to us. Focus on the Lord. Stay absorbed in God's word, not on the current problem,

God has that. Be thankful for the little things in life. They may seem tiny, but they are mighty and real.

Psalm 16:11 "Thou wilt shew me the path of life: in thy presence is fulness of joy; at thy right hand there are pleasures for evermore."

The love of Jesus abounds and knows no end. Christ cares for every one of us no matter who we are, what jobs we do or how our bank account looks. God is not prejudice concerning anything, not even the multitude of our concerns Perhaps someone at work is being rude, or maybe a trip from the doctor's office brings news, which seems devastating. Rest assured God knows, but he still wants supplications sent to him. He desires for us to turn it over to him completely.

Jesus Christ offers each of us the same salvation, and identical blessings. He shows equal rights in every way. It is up to us to cling to faith and trust in his able loving arms.

Galatians 3:28 "There is neither Jew nor Greek, there is neither bond nor free, there is neither male nor female: for ye are all one in Christ Jesus."

CHAPTER THREE

Turning our Troubles Over To God

Admit it; handing our worries over to the Lord isn't easy. We want to do things ourselves. I am sure, one time or another we all have been guilty of taking burdens back from God. Perhaps we simply forgot the importance of petitioning him wholeheartedly about our situation. Often impatience is the reason. We get tired of waiting on the Lord and forget that his time to move is not always what we want.

We may be scared that God's solution to our hardship will not please us. We need to step back and trust in Jesus. The outcome may not be our first choice, but it will fit into the Lord's plans.

Another major reason we pull our cares away from a loving God is that we over-think the problem. Our thoughts hinder us from trusting in the Lord. Mentally pondering on our woes will cause anxiety. It can make our imagination run in staggered paths and tromp on a peaceful day.

Leaving our cares in God's hands is a progression in faith that we build upon.

Surrendering our concerns to the Lord takes practice. Remember, learning to ride a bike? Once we achieved the goal, and mastered balancing the bicycle, peddling anywhere was easy.

The same principle applies to achieving harmony when a problem arises. As we wade through trials there are steps to take which by faith and belief offer a steadiness that forever will be embedded in our conscience, ready for us to remember the next time we encounter a hurdle.

Our thoughts will try to rule over us and doubt can begin to take root. The fretfulness will jump ahead of our serenity, all for the sake of enticing us to have a mental self-talk with ourselves about our problem. It is essential that we push those ideas away. Fast. Decide not to let the problem become the focus of the day. Sing a song, concentrate on the work at hand or start a project. Take away any chance of debating about the outcome of the situation. Place all notions back on the knowledge that Jesus Christ is hope and restoration for any dilemma.

Is it possible to rest in the Lord with practice and determination? Yes, but we must squash anxiety before it has a chance to take root in our mind and heart.

As humans our feelings come from our thoughts. If we change our thought process, then we modify the way we feel. At least the way we let our feelings reign over us.

God encourages us to focus on other things and let him shoulder our problems.

Colossians 3:2 "Set your affection on things above, not on things on the earth."

Matthew 6:34 "Take therefore no thought for the morrow: for the morrow shall take thought for the things of itself. Sufficient unto the day is the evil thereof."

A sure way to master turning our problems over to the Lord with ease is to be certain in his promises. As Christians, we are aware of the many assurances the Lord has given. Holding on to those declarations will chip away harmful ideas of doom and enable us to smile, even when our world seems like it is falling apart.

God offers wisdom when we need it.

James 1:5 "If any of you lack wisdom, let him ask of God, that giveth to all men liberally, and upbraideth not; and it shall be given him."

The Lord offers comfort.

2 Corinthians 1:3-4 "Blessed be God, even the Father of our Lord Jesus Christ, the Father of mercies, and the God of all comfort; Who comforteth us in all our tribulation, that we may be able to comfort them which are in any trouble, by the comfort wherewith we ourselves are comforted of God."

God has provided grace unmeasurable.

2 Corinthians 9:8 "And God is able to make all grace abound toward you; that ye, always having all sufficiency in all things, may abound to every good work:"

Our wonderful Heavenly Father gives us strength to withstand the trials we endure.

Philippians 4:13 "I can do all things through Christ which strengtheneth me."

Jesus Christ helps us remember that better things wait.

Romans 8:18 "For I reckon that the sufferings of this present time are not worthy to be compared with the glory which shall be revealed in us."

There are many more scriptures that are valuable in the Bible, there to minister to us in times of need. A good dose of these affirmations and prayer is sure to make our road smoother while we tread the often-rocky path that the world takes us down. Ask the Lord for strength. This helps to grow in trust, with assurance that God handles all needs.

Mark 9:23-24 Jesus said unto him, "If thou canst believe, all things are possible to him that believeth. And straightway the father of the child cried out, and said with tears, Lord, I believe; help thou mine unbelief."

A child of God can really have confidence. God will deliver us from the storm. Or lead each of us through the raging flood with favor and mercy, either way, the joy in the Lord will surpass all understanding.

Habakkuk 3:18 "Yet I will rejoice in the LORD, I will joy in the God of my salvation."

Psalm 35:9 "And my soul shall be joyful in the LORD: it shall rejoice in his salvation."

CHAPTER FOUR

The Lords knows, why ask?

Suppose a colleague sees peppermints on a co-workers desk. Maybe, they are used to enjoying one every day. Of course, no one minds sharing, but we all appreciate it if we are asked first, before someone helps themselves. It is the same way with the Lord. Yes, God knows all about the problems in our lives. He has knowledge of our thoughts and actions. Still, the Lord wants us to come to him in prayer and ask him for grace and guidance. To pray for mercy.

Prayer in a Christian's life is as vital as our heartbeat.

Petitioning the Lord is important, but believing in his promises is crucial. Jesus Christ makes the way and provides all of our needs and we must hold fast to that knowledge. Belief is also indispensable when it comes to receiving all that God has to offer.

Philippians 4:19 "But my God shall supply all your need according to his riches in glory by Christ Jesus."

The book of Acts is a good reinforcement for highlighting the significance of prayer in our lives. The disciples are a good example. They stayed dedicated to prayer and sought God in many ways for his leading.

Acts 2:24 "And they continued steadfastly in the apostles' doctrine and fellowship, and in breaking of bread, and in prayers."

Acts 3:1 "Now Peter and John went up together into the temple at the hour of prayer, being the ninth hour."

The disciples walked with Jesus but they depended on prayer. Praying is not about informing Jesus of our problems. It is about requesting and opening our hearts up to the Lord in submission to God. Just as a child comes to a parent with a request, the Lord wants his children to come to him and invite him into our lives, and our concerns.

Philippians 4:6 "Be careful for nothing; but in every thing by prayer and supplication with thanksgiving let your requests be made known unto God."

Jeremiah 33:3 "Call unto me, and I will answer thee, and shew thee great and mighty things, which thou knowest not."

When we go to the Lord in prayer, something else also happens. We have fellowship with him. Many of God's children talk to Jesus every day just as they do a friend. Indeed, Christ is our friend. The Lord assured us of this so that we will know he is everything to us in this turbulent world. As we go through our storms, the Lord guides us and offers comfort with an assurance that better things wait.

John 15:15 "Henceforth I call you not servants; for the servant knoweth not what his lord doeth: but I have called you friends; for all things that I have heard of my Father I have made known unto you."

God wants us to call on him. If we never go to the Lord in prayer, how would we grow stronger? Being on our knees is often the way to carry a heavy load with ease.

John 15:4 "Abide in me, and I in you. As the branch cannot bear fruit of itself, except it abide in the vine; no more can ye, except ye abide in me."

Praying to God, in Jesus' name, establishes a bond that man cannot break. It gives God an opportunity to use our problems for good. We always resent our troubles but we should realize that there are times that we look back and see how the Lord used a difficulty to mold us, either in faith or in grace.

Why prayer?

Our prayers are the way we hand the storms in our lives over to Jesus Christ. As we pray, we strengthen ourselves by placing trust in him. Taking burdens to Christ also shows him love and respect.

In all things have a dependable prayer life, it reinforces faith.

Jesus went to the cross for us; we are heirs in his kingdom. Christ wants to bless us and he likes us to turn to him for everything.

1 Corinthians 14:15 "What am I to do? I will pray with my spirit, but I will pray with my mind also; I will sing praise with my spirit, but I will sing with my mind also."

CHAPTER FIVE

Leave the Worry Behind

Easily said. Not so easily done.

A boomerang. That is how the situation can be as we practice giving our cares over to God. One day is awesome! The Lord has this. The next day a new development occurs with the problem and we pull it away from God's arms. As mentioned earlier casting our cares to the Lord is a process that takes a determined awareness.

Be humble. We are all used to fixing things ourselves. If something happens, our first instinct is to try to make things better. We need to humble ourselves especially with the Lord. A heart not puffed up is more inclined to turn everything over to Jesus Christ.

Humbleness really is obeying God, doing as the Lord says and having the right view of ourselves in relation to God.

The world would have us think that being humble is a weakness. God's word says to be meek is to not be proud with arrogance. Once we truly forget our egos, we will trust in God completely. That enables us to leave our cares in the Lord's hands for we know that God is bigger than our burden and he is in control.

James 4:10 "Humble yourselves in the sight of the Lord, and he shall lift you up."

Proverbs 29:23 "A man's pride shall bring him low: but honour shall uphold the humble in spirit."

Worship is the opposite of worry.

Make a determined decision to worship the Lord when worry tries to creep into our minds. Place the outcome with God and his supreme understanding. By deliberately turning worry into a "thank you Jesus," we flatten the worry into a pile and leave it behind while we step into an understanding that Jesus guides and provides for us.

Psalm 61:1, 2 "Hear my cry, O God; Give heed to my prayer. From the end of the earth I call to You when my heart is faint; Lead me to the rock that is higher than I."

CHAPTER SIX

The Roadmap to our Soul

All through this book, we have been made aware of how thoughts will rule over our emotions. When we focus on positive things, it increases our faith. Reflecting on the awesome power of the Father of light is encouraging and increases our belief in all the wondrous possibilities that the Lord has in store. An assured mind makes us able to take on the hardship in life with grace. A sure mindset also gives us inner strength when problems arise.

2 Corinthians 10:5 "Casting down imaginations, and every high thing that exalteth itself against the knowledge of God, and bringing into captivity every thought to the obedience of Christ;"

Proverbs 17:22 "A merry heart doeth good [like] a medicine: but a broken spirit drieth the bones."

Bad, hurtful and upsetting ideas try to hang onto us.

Imaginations about the worst possible outcome concerning the problems in our lives will plant themselves in our thoughts and wreak havoc with our faith. If we hang on to the worry, we soon find that our ability to believe in God's word dwindles. This will cause separation from the Lord and draw us away from the closeness we have with Jesus Christ. The only way to stop that harmful path in life is to cast it down with God's word. Reinforce all the negativity with good or with a scripture from the Bible that will relate to the situation.

Philippians 4:8 "Finally, brethren, whatsoever things are true, whatsoever things are honest, whatsoever things are just, whatsoever things are pure, whatsoever things are lovely, whatsoever things are of good report; if there be any virtue, and if there be any praise, think on these things."

It helps to reinforce good ideas by writing down scriptures about God's promise. Another aid is to jot a verse on a note card for strength and keep it close by. When a bad thought threatens to pull a concern back from the Lord, read the verse. Speak the verses in thought and reflect on them every time a concern creeps back and tries to take the day over.

Isaiah 40:31 "But they that wait upon the LORD shall renew [their] strength; they shall mount up with wings as eagles; they shall run, and not be weary; [and] they shall walk, and not faint."

Make a determined step not to take back the worry.

Refuse to let the problem dominate.

Focus on something other than the situation.

If we worked hard to keep the peace that Jesus offers and still have issues with finding harmony in times of trails, reaffirming our stand and not giving up is the next step.

Psalm 46:1 "God is our refuge and strength, an ever-present help in trouble."

Leaving our cares with Jesus is like learning to ride that bicycle. One push at a time and the next thing we know we are soaring through the tall grass, hardly noticing the weeds that scrape against our legs.

Proverbs 3:5-6 "Trust in the Lord with all thine heart; and lean not unto thine own understanding.

God will fix the problem, not us.

If worry becomes the center of attention we must focus on something beyond that burden, look ahead at the good things in life. This is not saying that we deny the heartache exists, but only that we are determined to center our hearts on better times ahead.

In certain situations, we have to remind ourselves that God is the answer to the problem. He will make a way. The most we can do is to entreat the Lord to continue and teach us how to have the grace we need to walk in the mist of the storm and to do it with calmness that we can only obtain with the Lord's help.

Turning over our burdens means that we make a conscious effort not to worry about it. Lean on God's promises and trust in his ways.

Our authority to control all the things we encounter is limited, but God's sovereignty to oversee our lives does not have a boundary. We must accept that fact and receive the peace that Jesus offers his children.

Jeremiah 29:11 "For I know the thoughts that I think toward you, saith the LORD, thoughts of peace, and not of evil, to give you an expected end."

At times, the outcome to our problems may not be what we want. It will hurt and cause us to question but God sees ahead. We all react to our feelings. That is why it is necessary to change the way we think. The things we ponder in our mind directly linked to our soul and to our health.

Matthew 15:18 "But those things which proceed out of the mouth come forth from the heart; and they defile the man."

The Lord knows each one of us. He understands that often the way we think can define our relationship with other people and with him because of this, it is important to guard our spirituality, especially in the bad times.

Philippians 2:5 "Let this mind be in you, which was also in Christ Jesus:"

CHAPTER SEVEN

Quality Time with Jesus

Quality time with Jesus successfully reroutes our minds away from negative, hindering thought patterns to a more positive outlook where we put our cares in God's hands and leave them there.

But how?

We all lead busy lives. Creating a close relationship with anyone takes time and so does having a special connection with the Lord but the desire alone does not do any good. Developing an important relationship with Jesus Christ has to become our priority.

It takes time to break old habits and establish new ones. Growing a closer walk with God is something we must purposely set out to do each day and we can make it more attainable by choosing times when our schedule is free from or attending to outside responsibilities.

One thing is sure, when we set out to expand on our relationship with Jesus Christ every type of distraction imaginable tries to block our path. This is when we need to ignore our cell phones and let the emails wait until later. The universe will still survive if we forego all these disruptions for a while. Concentrate on developing a closer relationship with God.

Make it a point every day to be mindful of the things that pull at time. Whether it is in the mornings, evenings or at night, take intervals and elect only to relax in God's presence. Purposely push other things away and spend time in God's word. A new habit of enjoying time with the Lord will emerge.

Just as we share our troubles with a pastor or a spouse, communicate with the Lord. Pray about burdens. Tell Jesus all the fears, and express to him the worries. After fretting, crying, and fussing over the injustice then meditate on God's word. The Bible offers promises and insights about any situation. No matter the problem, scriptures of deliverance are there for all to depend on. Now we are on the right track, growing in his presence and casting our cares his way with a stronger confidence

As we give our burdens to the Lord, we must pay attention to any negative thoughts that seep into the mind. We are to be on alert for ideas that will rob us from God's peace. Becoming aware of any harmful notions that the devil plants in our thoughts will help us push the hindrance away and trample his interference. Give the problem to the Lord, and believe.

John 17:15 "I pray not that thou shouldest take them out of the world, but that thou shouldest keep them from the evil."

Pesky notions introduced by the devil will try to make us believe that things are hopeless. Never the less, hope is not lost. A child of God is blessed in many ways.

Isaiah 26:3, 4 "You keep him in perfect peace whose mind is stayed on you, because he trusts in you. Trust in the LORD forever, for the LORD GOD is an everlasting rock."

2 Corinthians 1:10, 11"He delivered us from such a deadly peril, and he will deliver us. On him we have set our hope that he will deliver us again. You also must help us by prayer, so that many will give thanks on our behalf for the blessing granted us through the prayers of many."

CHAPTER EIGHT

Believe

Believe is such a straightforward word. The Merriam-Webster Dictionary sites many varieties of meaning. The simple significance of believe is to accept or regard (something) as true or to accept the truth of what is said by someone.

One of the definitions of the intransitive verb for believing means to have a firm religious faith. That expression far expands anything the dictionaries or internet can define.

When we use the word, "believe" in a spiritual context we are speaking about much more than agreeing that God's word is true.

Christians trust and have faith in our Heavenly Father and are committed to serving the Lord in the way our understanding directs.

Yes, we have faith in the Lord Jesus Christ. We believe his promises, but believing also means we trust enough to follow his leading and to obey his teachings.

John 14:15 "If ye love me, keep my commandments."

We must also have an inner confidence that can't be shaken by the world or by any problems that we may encounter.

Proverbs 3:6 "In all thy ways acknowledge him, and he shall direct thy paths.

To have unwavering belief we must stand strong in our faith. This furnishes us with the fortitude to cast our cares upon the Lord and leave them there.

Create somewhat of a schedule to make the time to get into God's word. Don't push to read entire books of the Bible in one setting, but do put aside time to study a few scriptures or verses of the Lord's wonderful roadmap to salvation.

A great way to increase the ability to leave cares with Jesus is to write out prayers. Maybe start a journal scribing concerns and jotting down scriptures that offer solutions.

Devotionals are a wonderful way to intensify our ability to rely on the Lord. A testimony of how someone battled a similar problem often backs those short stories. The way the writers' witness to their faith seals the knowledge of the importance of resting on the peace that Jesus instills.

Another great way to lean solely on the verse of 1 Peter 5:7 is to act upon all the scriptures. Walk the Christian pathway with determination to follow Jesus. Regardless of our woes, we need to talk with faith in every situation. A priority in all we do is to recognize annoying thoughts of doubt that placed in our minds by the devil. These ideas are from a worldly prospective, they are not the final word that is according to our loving God.

The verse in 1 Peter tells us, in no uncertain terms, to cast our cares. We as Christians should strive each day to live by God's words and the nudges the Holy Spirit provides. However, the world, the adversary and all the distractions would like nothing more but to have us waver in all our ways. Jesus warns us about being tossed about by our emotions.

James 1:6 "But let him ask in faith, nothing wavering. For he that wavereth is like a wave of the sea driven with the wind and tossed."

The Lord is the believer's stronghold. He is our salvation here, while we are in this world and in the world to come. God does care for us. He proved that many years ago with the cross. Relying on him in times of sorrow give us an opportunity to know that he'll demonstrate his love again and again.

Romans 15:13 "Now the God of hope fill you with all joy and peace in believing, that ye may abound in hope, through the power of the Holy Ghost."

CHAPTER NINE

The Lord Uses Problems for His Glory

It is hard to go through trials and heartache. We sometimes wonder "why." We examine our life. We question God. With many things, there is no earthly answer, but there is a divine response that one day we will understand.

The Lord loves us and is always willing to be our guiding light. Through tough circumstances, he molds us so that we will have a closer walk with him. Only God can take bad situations and turn them into something to use for our good and his glory.

Problems can make us re-think our life.

We can become complacent with our spiritual walk. If an uneasy situation makes us contemplate change, then perhaps God used that rocky road to move us in another direction.

Problems can make us draw nigh to the Lord. Maybe, we had grown stale and stopped moving toward our Heavenly Father the way we did when we were first saved. God will quicken our spirit and let us know that we need to develop closeness with him again. Once we realize that we can get back on the right track. Then when the next battle comes our way, we know that we will be dressed in the armor of the Lord.

Proverbs 3:5-6 "Trust in the LORD with all your heart; and lean not upon your own understanding. In all your ways acknowledge him, and he shall direct your path."

Troubles can bring out the best or the worst in a person.

Sometimes a burden will make us realize that our trust in God has weakened. The Lord will direct our focus, so we can clearly see the lack that has robbed us of peace. His word will establish in us a new awareness, which promises to increase the trust we need to have joy in the Lord during all the things good or bad. With that new awakening, our faith becomes sharper.

James 1:2-3 "My brethren, count it all joy when ye fall into divers temptations; Knowing this, that the trying of your faith worketh patience."

The reasons hardships happen are many. Stories are told of people not being where they wanted to be due to a car problem. Passengers have missed their flights because of simple delays in their schedules. Numerous times an unfortunate situation befalls someone, and later they discovered it was for the best. The Lord works amongst chaos to show his children that he is in control.

2 Thessalonians 3:3 "But the Lord is faithful, who shall stablish you, and keep you from evil."

When we stand in front of burdens, we often get disillusioned.

Reading Psalms we find out that David endured many problems. Some were from the effects of situations that he deliberately caused, others happened because of prejudice. Through all that David dealt with, he still honored the Lord. Regardless, David continued to trust God.

Psalm 86:5 "For thou, Lord, art good, and ready to forgive; and plenteous in mercy unto all them that call upon thee."

David was faithful and depended on God with all his heart, even when he walked in trouble.

Psalm 18:2 "The Lord is my rock, and my fortress, and my deliverer; my God, my strength, in whom I will trust; my buckler, and the horn of my salvation, and my high tower."

As with King David, we face bad times, but be assured that our Savior is using them to help us reach a higher spiritual level.

Looking beyond a crisis can be difficult. Still, we know that the Lord will make a way. Whatever we must walk through will work to make us a stronger Christian, if we stand fast and continue to trust and believe.

Indeed, the road we travel is determined by the way we handle our problems. A life mapped out from casting our concerns to the Lord is an existence that guarantees we will have the peace that only comes from the Lord.

Psalm 46:11 "The Lord of hosts is with us; the God of Jacob is our refuge. Selah."

CHAPTER TEN

Apostle Paul and Colossians 3:23

Paul, who called himself an apostle of Christ Jesus, lived the last part of his life working for the Lord bringing gentiles into Christianity. Before his transformation into a soldier for the Lord, he was Saul, a man who committed murder.

Saul, who later became Paul, could be classified as an extreme person. Everything he did seemed to be taken to a higher level than normal. Hate and violence filled the beginning of Saul's adult life. He did everything in his power to stop Christianity. Many people killed by his hands or because of his decrees. He tormented many God loving people and their children.

However, one day Saul was traveling the road to Damascus and a bright light prevented him from going any further. Saul cradled toward the ground as a voice from God called out to him. That day changed Saul forever. He became Paul, a new person who willingly went about working for the Lord and spreading the gospel.

Acts 9:3-6 "And as he journeyed, he came near Damascus: and suddenly there shined round about him a light from heaven: And he fell to the earth, and heard a voice saying unto him, Saul, Saul, why persecutest thou me? And he said, Who art thou, Lord? And the Lord said, I am Jesus whom thou persecutest: it is hard for thee to kick against the pricks. And he trembling and astonished said, Lord, what wilt thou have me to do? And the

Lord said unto him, Arise, and go into the city, and it shall be told thee what thou must do."

Paul continued into Damascus, and a disciple named Ananias gave him the rest of the Lord's message. That day Paul became an apostle.

The word "apostle" means messenger or someone sent to carry out a word. He was baptized as a follower of Christ Jesus.

Perhaps the intense personality Paul had was one reason God chose him to become the apostle to the Gentiles. Paul went on to use his enthusiasm for the Lord, even though he suffered much during his travels.

Colossians is a Prison Epistle or simply a letter Paul wrote while he was in jail. The complete book written by Paul was in response to the unorthodox teachings. Also, it was written to motivate, and inspire believers to serve with commitment.

In chapter 3, Paul is reassuring the church to focus on God and the things above (3:2). He addressed Christians, leading them on ways to attend to their personal matters and gave suggestions about fellowshipping with one another. Paul offered guidance so that they would stay focused on the Lord. One worthy verse is in Colossians 3: 23.

Colossians 3:23 "And whatsoever ye do, do it heartily, as to the Lord, and not unto men;"

Anyone familiar with this scripture knows it carries an important message. We can study this passage but to apply the verse to our lives requires a bit of fortitude, especially when we are called upon to help in times that we have other projects demanding our attention.

Paul writes to the Colossians, "And whatever you do." a reminder that in all things we do to respect our task. God likes his children to attend to their days as a dutiful caretaker.

Jesus serves, so can we.

One of the most important parts of Paul's scripture says "as to the Lord and not to men." This is often difficult because families and others will call upon us, pulling us in all directions. It's hard to keep smiling when the feelings of pressured to serve gets in the way. Still, the Lord wants us to carry out our duties heartily, with our whole-heart and not begrudge the task.

It is nice to make people happy, but the focus during these times needs to be on serving the Lord the way the scriptures says, and not man.

Each day as we consider our jobs, and other duties we need to aspire to serve the best we can, with a happy heart. The Lord will reward us. It may not be on the same day that we do a good deed but God will bless us. In all, we need to choose to satisfy our Heavenly Father and our promise of an eternal life.

CHAPTER ELEVEN

Tend to Things Heartily

It is imperative that we keep the joy of the Lord with everything our hands touch. We must have Christian characteristics.

Galatians 5:22-23 "But the fruit of the Spirit is love, joy, peace, longsuffering, gentleness, goodness, faith, Meekness, temperance: against such there is no law."

Romans 12:2 "And be not conformed to this world: but be ye transformed by the renewing of your mind, that ye may prove what is that good, and acceptable, and perfect, will of God."

Everyone has a busy life. We have jobs, kids, church activities and social events that keep us running. There are times when we hardly have time to eat right because we are busy running to tend to the things on our schedules. Perhaps, someone commented on a project. Maybe they mentioned that the task was finished. Still, it turned out to be a half-hearted duty. That was their admission that they did the chore without enthusiasm and only went through the motions to get it finished. If we remember what Colossians says, then we must realize that we are not living up to the Lord's standards if we do not fulfill the job with a willing heart.

Attending to all our pursuits with joy is vital. We should oversee everything as if we are doing the job for Jesus. We need to forget that we are working for an employer. We are to manage our responsibilities as if we work for the Lord.

Yes, we get a paycheck, but when we put our all into what we do, a heavenly reward awaits.

The Lord is the one who will compensate us in the end, not the employer. The financial reward from our employer is good but money will not get us to heaven. The Kingdom of Heaven is our inheritance, not what we gain while on earth.

Hebrews 10:36 "For ye have need of patience, that, after ye have done the will of God, ye might receive the promise."

Whether it's a spiritual job, a high-profile career, helping a neighbor or painting, we need to do our best and care about the job we are involved with.

Being able to glorify the Lord in all we do is an awesome quality for any Christian to nourish.

CHAPTER TWELVE

Keep an Enthusiastic Attitude

We may not consider the errands we do for others or the career we have as an activity that God has placed in our lives. Any vocation we encounter is to be for his purpose. In our duties, we may get a chance to witness to someone. Whether we hold a position in management or we are helpers for a day we need to attend to it with a God like attitude.

In addition, we should never discount the fact that the world is watching us as we come and go. People notice the way others act, especially Christians. Some will stand back and observe just to see how a child of God reacts to everyday situations.

Often one of the best witnessing that we do for the glory of the Lord is in silence, through our actions. God's children have a light of mercy that shines and makes people take notice. Cultivating a determined mindset to have the joy of the Lord and be happy in all our pursuits will get us to a place where we will be an illuminating representative for the kingdom of God.

If we make a point to be content in everything we do then we develop a sincere outlook in all our undertakings.

Here are a few Bible verses that will encourage us keep a positive frame of mind as well as reinforce the promise of a glorious forever.

Philippians 2:5 "Let this mind be in you, which was also in Christ Jesus."

Proverbs 17:22 "A merry heart doeth good [like] a medicine: but a broken spirit drieth the bones."

Colossians 3:17 'And whatsoever ye do in word or deed, [do] all in the name of the Lord Jesus, giving thanks to God and the Father by him."

Ephesians 4:31 "Let all bitterness, and wrath, and anger, and clamor, and evil speaking, be put away from you, with all malice."

Romans 5:1-2 "Therefore being justified by faith, we have peace with God through our Lord Jesus Christ: By whom also we have access by faith into this grace wherein we stand, and rejoice in hope of the glory of God."

CHAPTER THIRTEEN

The Devil's Tricks—-God's Treats

Satan lives to try his best to rule us. If he can plant a bad thought in our minds about a friend, make us believe a lie, or get us involved in the latest office gossip then the adversary smiles because he has brought us to his level.

1 Peter 5 "Be sober, be vigilant; because your adversary the devil, as a roaring lion, walketh about, seeking whom he may devour."

None of us is perfect. Paul says in 1 Corinthians 15:13 that he dies daily. We are no better than Paul is. Living in a sinful world even the best Christian is bound to get flustered and say, think, or do something that is against what a child of God stands for. We must not give up because of a slip that caused us to step away from the glory of the Lord for a second, but we do have to repent and resolve to be a better person in our stand for the Lord.

Satan enjoys putting things in our path that will make us begrudge certain obligations. We should be on the lookout for ways, which the evil one uses to place us in a bad frame of mind. The adversary wants to make us forget that our daily missions should be done for the glory of God and not man.

Satan is the master of manipulation. His purpose is to turn us away from doing the will of God. He gets pleasure from planting barricades in front of us and putting distance between Jesus Christ and us. In John, the scriptures tell a bit about his ugly character.

John 10:10 "The thief cometh not, but for to steal, and to kill, and to destroy: I am come that they might have life, and that they might have it more abundantly."

Tricks are the devil's trademark. He has used them for hundreds of years. Nevertheless, we can still fall prey to his interference. He likes to use the sinful ways in the world to trap us in ungodly situations. He will entice us and temporarily blind, us from following God's will. It is of upmost importance that we stay focused on God's word so that we stay in tune to the warning signs.

Satan has several habits he hangs on to, geared to make us forget that all we do should be for God's glory. His main strategy is to plant ideas or objections in our mind.

He will challenge God's Word.

At times, we all have defended the Holy word. The devil will put people in our path that will raise questions or cause controversy concerning the passages in the Bible. As we should, as Christians, we will support God's word but the devil uses this in two ways.

Satan's reasons for doing this are to hinder someone's salvation and to attempt to interject thoughts of doubt in our minds. The evil one wants to make us uncertain about our Heavenly Father's messages. These obstacles are in our path in hopes to cause us to abandon the many way-making verses. If the devil can construct a smidgen of doubt about God's word it influences everything we do and lets the importance of doing for others slide to the wayside.

The devil is a good imitator. He will use passages from the Bible for his purposes. One of the verses that come to mind is in Matthew where it says that we are to do unto others as we would want them to do to us. How many of us have heard someone quote it incorrectly and comment, "Do unto others as they do unto you?"

Matthew 7:12 "Therefore all things whatsoever ye would that men should do to you, do ye even so to them: for this is the law and the prophets."

That's certainly not what God's word says but if people hear that enough and don't read the verse with a watchful eye, they could come to believe it to be so, and not fully understand that the scripture is instructing for us to treat others the way we want them to treat us.

Satan enjoys getting us into a prideful mindset.

Pride will make us focus on ourselves and draw our attention away from God's suggestions that we are to help each other.

1 Timothy 3:6 "Not a novice, lest being lifted up with pride he fall into the condemnation of the devil."

If we let pride grow roots, we will eventually put ourselves above others. Pride is the reverse of love and puts us into a place where we can become impatient, unfriendly and selfish. The Holy Spirit knows this a weapon of evil and warns us concerning it.

2 Timothy 3:1-2 "This know also, that in the last days perilous times shall come. For men shall be lovers of their own selves,

covetous, boasters, proud, blasphemers, disobedient to parents, unthankful, unholy,"

Envy is another arrow the devil will use.

If Satan can turn us toward envy for other things then he has pricked us with a feeling that the world is unfair. We will begin to begrudge our tasks. Eventually we may become puffed up and tell ourselves, "We deserve better than to be servants to our neighbors."

James 3:16King James Version "For where envying and strife is, there is confusion and every evil work."

Satan enjoys placing a spirit of dissatisfaction on us.

He knows if he can catch a Christian at a weak point, disappointment can make us compare ourselves to others and we will become disheartened. Discouragement puts us in a self-absorbed mood. While the adversary has us feeling dissatisfied we focused on ourselves, and forget the importance of lending a hand to others.

It is a "poor me" attitude.

Satan bottles this mindset, puts a fancy label on it and administers it to all who he can trick into turning their eyes away from the teachings of Jesus Christ. Good people can be crippled by the poor-me syndrome.

Life is full of disappointments.

Satan uses every opportunity to use our failures to his advantage. If we dwell on everything that we consider a malfunction in life then we will become discouraged.

One widely used device from the evil one is disbelief.

The devil works daily to install uncertainty in us concerning others. He wants to make us hesitant about God's word and confound us. By keeping us in a state of bewilderment, Satan hides the promises of God under a blanket of confusion. Again, that is his way of trying to rule over our thoughts.

Philippians 2:5 "Let this mind be in you, which was also in Christ Jesus."

The devil uses many things to sway us away from doing good deeds and following the teachings of Jesus Christ. He will do anything to keep our minds busy with worldly concerns, doubt and frustration to draw us away from all the Lord seeks us to be.

In all the trails, we cross we must remember the Bible is our roadmap while we are here on earth. God's word maps out a route. If we follow it we will be led to blessings, and a joyous eternity.

Scriptures to help keep us smile when we have wearisome tasks.

We would not be human if we didn't have days when we struggle with keeping a good attitude while working or being a help mate to others. Here are a few scriptures to ponder on when things get to be trying.

Matthew 5:16 "Let your light so shine before men, that they may see your good works, and glorify your Father which is in heaven."

Hebrews 6:10 "For God is not unjust so as to overlook your work and the love that you have shown for his name in serving the saints, as you still do."

Luke 22:27 "For who is the greater, one who reclines at table or one who serves? Is it not the one who reclines at table? But I am among you as the one who serves."

Romans 12:10-11 "Love one another with brotherly affection. Outdo one another in showing honor. Do not be slothful in zeal, be fervent in spirit, serve the Lord."

Matthew 5:42 "Give to him that asketh thee, and from him that would borrow of thee turn not thou away."

James 2:14-17 "What doth it profit, my brethren, though a man say he hath faith, and have not works? Can faith save him? If a brother or sister be naked, and destitute of daily food, And one of you say unto them, Depart in peace, be ye warmed and filled; notwithstanding ye give them not those things which are needful to the body; what doth it profit? Even so faith, if it hath not works, is dead, being alone."

Every word in the Bible is important. God's word holds insight, which benefits us all. A verse that we may have only read and not given much thought to can one day become a way-making scripture of grace in our lives.

We have all heard that God's word is as pertinent in life today as it was a century ago. That is so true, and the longer we live the clearer that knowledge becomes.

CHAPTER FOURTEEN

Push Satan Away

Satan, the devil, the adversary or the enemy, no matter what we call him, he is evil. His sole purpose is to place hardships in our lives and deliver discouragement. His major focus is to hinder our thoughts. All this is an attempt to turn us away from the Lord and make everything in our lives ugly.

Even Jesus was not immune. Satan tempted Jesus to show his great power and tried to entice Christ with riches. He was desperate to use anything to sway Jesus from his destination. (Matthew 4:1-10) Our awesome Savior stood firm and fought Satan with God's word.

Matthew 4:11"Then saith Jesus unto him, Get thee hence, Satan: for it is written, Thou shalt worship the Lord thy God, and him only shalt thou serve."

The temptation on the mountain, which Jesus fought, can be our first lesson on ways to push the devil's interference away. Notice that with every one of the lures Satan used Jesus countered it with God's word. He specifically said, "It is written."

For Jesus the main purpose of his life was to please our Heavenly Father and bring us salvation. The enemy tried countless times to tempt Jesus to sin, but Christ was always ready to give Satan the truth in the written word. He fought with powerful lifesaving words, as we should do.

To be strong in battle against evil we must surround ourselves with worship and have knowledge of God's way-making scriptures. Victory will be ours providing we have a Monday through Saturday relationship with God and not just a Sunday visit. Being familiar with the scriptures in the Bible is important. Not only do we grow in the understanding of our Lord, but we also fill our minds with ammunition to use on Satan when he comes at us.

Another way to keep the devil at arm's length is to head to the writings in Ephesians. Paul makes a point to instruct every Christian about the magnitude of walking in righteousness. He reveals an example of how being holy can help to stop his interference.

Ephesians 4:26 "Be ye angry, and sin not: let not the sun go down upon your wrath:"

If we put ourselves into positions that produce iniquity, we are partying with the enemy. Satan takes this as an invitation to set up resistance or attack us.

Paul wants us to realize that by letting anger linger in our minds we open ourselves up to an attack from the enemy. To be a strong Christian we need to hand out forgiveness as soon as possible. This closes the door to the adversary before he has a chance to use our weakness against us.

Speaking malice about someone may not seem bad but it lets Satan cross over the blood of Jesus into our path.

Romans 1:30-32 "Backbiters, haters of God, despiteful, proud, boasters, inventors of evil things, disobedient to parents, Without understanding, covenant breakers, without natural affection, implacable, unmerciful: Who knowing the judgment of God, that they which commit such things are worthy of death, not only do the same, but have pleasure in them that do them."

God's word speaks about many intolerable doings that we can fall prey to which will move us farther from the Lord and closer to the enemy's camp. Obtaining things wrongfully, giving an unfavorable opinion about someone, or telling lies are a few. There are many types of sins. Playing with any sin, whether big or small is like shining a flashlight to light the way so that the devil can find his way into our life.

Matthew7:1"Judge not, that ye be not judged."

This verse from the book of James. As mentioned before. It is a passage, which is widely quoted.

James 4:7 "Submit yourselves therefore to God. Resist the devil, and he will flee from you."

Do we practice it with the authority infused in the words?

This verse is probably one of those stanzas we enjoy remembering but never give the credit due. It plainly tells us to submit to God. Resist the devil.

Obeying the Lord, following his teachings and presenting ourselves in a manner, which the Lord expects is equal to surrendering to God. If we walk each day in God's light and hold ourselves to a high standard being Christ-like, then the devil will flee. If he tries to tangle us in his snares then bring to remembrance that God's word plainly tells us to "resist." Stand firm and tell evil flee in the name of Jesus. The Bible tell us that even evil knows the power of our almighty Savior.

James 2:19 "Thou believest that there is one God; thou doest well: the devils also believe, and tremble."

There's one verse in the Bible that unmistakably outlines the route to take that will ward off Satan's attempts to control your life, it's in Ephesians.

Ephesians 6:11"Put on the whole armour of God, that ye may be able to stand against the wiles of the devil."

Ephesians 6:11 is perfectly clear. Christians are attacked by the wiles of the evil one every day and we must armor ourselves with the weapons God gave us when we accepted salvation. The suit that Paul refers to (Ephesians 6:13-17) is to have your loins girt about with truth, along with the breastplate of righteousness. Your feet shod with preparation of the gospel of peace. We are to carry the shield of faith, the helmet of salvation and the sword of the Spirit. Believers understand that we fight principalities and spiritually evil powers

Have your loins girt about with truth.

In the Roman days, the solders would pull their garment close and tie it with a belt to protect parts of their body. Paul reminds Christians to shelter themselves from anything that will cause stumbling within our religious walk. We must be mentally alert.

John 14:6 "Jesus saith unto him, I am the way, the truth, and the life: no man cometh unto the Father, but by me."

John 17:17 "Sanctify them through thy truth: thy word is truth."

The breastplate of Righteousness.

Ancient warriors used a breastplate for covering. It offered protection to the torso guarding important organs such as the heart and lungs. We have Jesus as our covering.

Without Christ, none of us would be righteous. Jesus is the honorable and virtuous one. God gives us victory through him. (1 Corinthians 15:57)

In addition to our Lord's mercy, we must dress ourselves with his protective breastplate, walking in faith and love.

1 Thessalonians 5:8 "But let us, who are of the day, be sober, putting on the breastplate of faith and love; and for an helmet, the hope of salvation."

Your feet shod with the preparation of the gospel of peace.

We wear shoes to protect our feet and help us walk on all types of terrain. Therefore, Christians must stand on the truth of the gospel. While we go about each day tending to our responsibilities, we need to walk with the teachings of Jesus and carry our faith to others. The Lord desires all to come to his knowledge.

1 Timothy 2:2-4 "For kings, and for all that are in authority; that we may lead a quiet and peaceable life in all godliness and

honesty. For this is good and acceptable in the sight of God our Savior; Who will have all men to be saved, and to come unto the knowledge of the truth."

Take the shield of faith.

When we think about a shield, we picture a big medal orb lifted in times of battle. Simply holding the shield will not accomplish anything. For it to be effective, it needs to be in a placed in a way that offers protection. Just like the shield that guards, faith is what protects our spiritual life.

The devil is forever throwing darts filled with uncertainty and anxiety. It is crucial to remember to hold tight to our shield of faith. God is on our side. If we keep in mind that the Lord always has our backs then faith becomes our unfillable defense in any situation.

Hebrews 11:1 "Now faith is the substance of things hoped for, the evidence of things not seen."

Think about this scripture for a second. "Faith is the substance of things hoped for." Substance is an ingredient that fits into any calculation. Evidence is proof. Faith is not just a feel good mood but it is an unquestionable, undeniable certainty.

Faith is truth, but for many people having faith does not come easy. Confidence in God's word has to be cultivated. It begins by trusting in the Lord and in his promises. It takes faith to accept salvation. The same principle applies to other areas of our life. We must hold to faith and believe, no matter what.

Helmet of salvation

Helmets are very important. When we ride a motorcycle, we wear a helmet. Fire fighters use protective gear to cover up. A defensive covering to protect the head is normal anytime in a challenging situation. It is not surprising that Paul directs us to wear a helmet to protect our salvation.

When we repent and become a child of God, we begin a new life. At that point, the devil has lost a soul.

Satan begins to attack, hoping to draw us away from our newfound redemption. He uses the same tactics on everyone. The devil will strike at a believer's confidence to create reasons to cause discouragement. He uses our past mistakes against us in the hope that we will feel unworthy to be a child of God. Satan will try to make us focus on our problems in an attempt to convince any Christian that we will never be good enough for our Heavenly Father. All these lies are designed to keep us in his realm, away from a loving God. No matter what thoughts Satan tries to plant, remember the Lord saves and in his sight we are worthy.

John 5:24 "Verily, verily, I say unto you, He that heareth my word, and believeth on him that sent me, hath everlasting life, and shall not come into condemnation; but is passed from death unto life."

Salvation is deliverance from sin and a promise of a heavenly eternal home. We are saved, and sanctified, by Jesus Christ.

John 10:28 "And I give unto them eternal life; and they shall never perish, neither shall any man pluck them out of my hand."

The sword of the Spirit

A sword is for both offensive and defensive moves. The "sword of the Spirit" is a weapon given to us by the Holy Spirit through God's word. The Bible is our defense.

Christians are on a spiritual crusade battling against the principalities of evil. We cannot avoid this path. We are to use God's word as a light and as a weapon against wickedness.

2 Corinthians 10:4-5 "For the weapons of our warfare are not carnal, but mighty through God to the pulling down of strong holds; Casting down imaginations, and every high thing that exalteth itself against the knowledge of God, and bringing into captivity every thought to the obedience of Christ;"

One of the reasons the Bible is written is to give us the firepower to stop Satan's ambushes. Just as Jesus used God's word to combat the devil we must keep the holy road map to salvation in our minds at all times so we can conquer evils. "It is written," is a motto a believer lives by.

The Holy Spirit also gives us strength to be a help to our brothers and sisters in Christ. Words that minister to others in their time of weaknesses will carry them to safety and reinforce faith.

Matthew 5:16 "Let your light so shine before men, that they may see your good works, and glorify your Father which is in heaven."

We touched on the subject of Satan's most used weapon, the way he tries to influence us through our thoughts. This arsenal is so sneaky that we need to look at it again.

Mind control

This sounds sinister, like something right out of a movie. When we think about this, we realize that it is as disturbing as it sounds. Satan is evil and stops at nothing to get a child of God to stumble. If he cannot make us fall, then he will hamper our mindset by infusing anything negative. Satan does this to weaken our faith. He throws out ideas that make us question our salvation. The adversary uses others to bring about uncertainty and cause us to second-guess our beliefs. He is the king of manipulation and wickedness.

When we walk with the Lord, we have a responsibility to stay in the path that Jesus paved. There is no diamond, pearl, or status in this life, that means more than the future we have as a child of God.

Philippians 4:8 "Finally, brethren, whatsoever things are true, whatsoever things are honest, whatsoever things are just, whatsoever things are pure, whatsoever things are lovely, whatsoever things are of good report; if there be any virtue, and if there be any praise, think on these things."

Control the things the devil tries to sneak past our defenses.

We can push discouraging notions aside and send him away by focusing on things that are pure and holy, just as the scripture tells us to do.

Another way to help ward off the plans of the devil is to spend time with people who love the Lord. Attending church and various events, which glorify God, is more than just something we should do. It is a way to fill up our faith tank. Gathering with other brothers and sisters in Christ supplies us with the fuel we need to step out into the workweek and attend our daily duties with a renewed encouragement.

1 Thessalonians 5:11"Wherefore comfort yourselves together, and edify one another, even as also ye do."

Be reassurance, our walk with the Lord is worth everything.

Things of this world can be enticing. Money, status and material wealth will try to blind us from the real goal of life. All the material possessions and the financial accounts we hold, or the praise from others will fade away. We cannot take any of these worldly favors with us when we die. Everyone has a time to leave this world. The only thing we will be able to carry with us is our souls.

Is our soul good or bad?

We can hide our true selves from others, but we will never be able to conceal what is in our heart from God.

CHAPTER FIFTEEN

Christ-like wisdom

Proverbs 1:7 "The fear of the Lord is the beginning of knowledge: but fools despise wisdom and instruction."

Fear has many different meanings. The word is widely known to represent a person being scared. It notates feelings of worry because of something dangerous or threatening. The term "fear" also has another meaning. It means to show respect and admiration.

Most children do not fear their mother or father, but when they are told to do their chores or to not to do something then they will obey because they understand the consequences if they fail to listen. This is similar to having fear for the Lord. As a Christian, we want to obey God's word because of the wonderful outcome that our Lord promises his children who abide by his commandments.

A new Christian could interpret Proverbs 1:7 to mean that we must be afraid of the Lord, but that is not what is conveyed. Here the term "fear of God" is to be a positive frame of mind. It should not be scary. God is the Almighty. He is our redeemer, forgiver of sins and savior. Having knowledge of the Lord is to reverence his power.

As believers, we need to follow the teachings of Jesus Christ, knowing that if not, we will miss a wonderful opportunity to have blessings and an abundant life.

Parents want to guide the little ones to a bright future. Out of love, they put restrictions on them. Christ loves us and wants us walk in his light, using his teachings as a guide to be Christ-like.

Revelation 3:19 "As many as I love, I rebuke and chasten: be zealous therefore, and repent."

The world will not agree that the Bible is the guide for life. They will not accept that God's words are a beacon that leads to eternity, but Christians understand this to be so.

Proverbs 14:26 "In the fear of the LORD [is] strong confidence: and his children shall have a place of refuge."

God's word is the beginning of wisdom.

Many people in this world are book smart and wise in numerous ways. However, wisdom in God's realm is not the same thing as having a worldly knowledge.

The Bible speaks of wisdom as having spiritual smarts and walking with God. Biblical insight aligns with God's plans and is in tune to the scriptures. A person does not need to know the complete Bible to be wise in God's eyes, but they should be an avid reader of the Holy book and a follower after righteousness, willing to seek God's word for direction.

Colossians 3:16 "Let the word of Christ dwell in you richly in all wisdom; teaching and admonishing one another in psalms and hymns and spiritual songs, singing with grace in your hearts to the Lord."

Godly wisdom is often mocked because it goes against a worldly nature. This outlook takes God's word and treats it with contempt, abhorring anything that is of instruction that does not create a monetary value. Some may never understand the true wisdom in the scriptures because of blind eyes and deaf ears. The world will have you to believe that God's wisdom holds no value, but believers have a better understanding, assured that this is the key to life ever after.

John 17:3"And this is life eternal, that they might know thee the only true God, and Jesus Christ, whom thou hast sent."

The Lord desires everyone to come to accept the everlasting life that he offers.

2 Peter 3:9 "The Lord is not slack concerning his promise, as some men count slackness; but is longsuffering to us-ward, not willing that any should perish, but that all should come to repentance."

We Christians must pray for one another so that we all will have an abundance of spiritual forethought.

Spiritual wisdom

James 3:13-18 "Who is a wise man and endued with knowledge among you? Let him shew out of a good conversation his works with meekness of wisdom. But if ye have bitter envying and strife in your hearts, glory not, and lie not against the truth. This wisdom descendeth not from above, but is earthly, sensual, devilish. For where envying and strife is, there is confusion and every evil work. But the wisdom that is from above is first pure, then peaceable, gentle, and easy to be intreated, full of mercy and good fruits, without partiality, and without hypocrisy. And the fruit of righteousness is sown in peace of them that make peace."

James does a wonderful job of outlining the essence of spiritual wisdom, but the importance of the word "wisdom," should not be overlooked. Wisdom not only means to be knowledgeable but it also notes someone who is wise in word and deed. In the book of James, he encourages us to use good judgment and to layer our lives with the wisdom that God expects his children to have.

It is not about the book smarts we acquire, or the degree hanging on the wall. It concerns the way each of us live and the responses we have to situations, which cross our path. Notice the words James uses are "peaceable, gentle, and full of mercy, without hypocrisy." Those qualities come from having a desire to, above all things. Please the Lord.

These characteristics are all conditions that should influence the way we deal with others.

Divine understanding entails studying to understand God's words. Spiritual awareness also means walking in this world each day while using the Bible as our standard.

Spiritual mindfulness is applying the teachings of Jesus Christ to everyday life.

It is difficult when personalities mix. Whether it is in a work environment, a social meeting, a worship assembly or a get-together, these activities often test our spiritual wisdom.

Worship assemblies are the totem pole of all events that can check our Godly wisdom. Everyone who comes together to praise the Lord is included in the family of God. All the differences in opinions can often make for disagreements. Walking in God's understanding is important. We must learn to use spiritual wisdom with each other when we come together. Forget placing blame for something that did not go perfect. Practice turning the other cheek at off-handed comments, remembering that we are all in different stages of understanding.

No situation is free from becoming a testing ground in the humbleness God expects his children to impart. No church is unflawed. The buildings we use to praise the Lord in are filled with a congregation that can never be complete, until Jesus Christ comes.

People will drop out of attending worship assemblies because of something someone said, or a situation that did not fall into a perceived notion. If we hold onto problems such as these, we are in danger of stunting our own spiritual growth. Can we show spiritual wisdom to the world and please God if we cannot get along with our brothers and sisters in church?

That question is often pushed aside. Without remembering what the Lord wants from us, we sometimes place blame and overlook the fact that we need to make a conscious decision to apply spiritual fruits in every circumstance to grow more Christ-like.

Hebrews 10:25 "Not forsaking the assembling of ourselves together, as the manner of some [is]; but exhorting [one another]: and so much the more, as ye see the day approaching."

Matthew 18:20 "For where two or three are gathered together in my name, there am I in the midst of them."

Just as most of us would not quit a job over a mishap, we should never give up being involved in a church because of indifferences. Worship centers are where we grow in faith and gather strength. Church is where we hear testimonies. These declarations about the Lord's goodness encourage us. We should never turn away from joining others in God's house. It is an honor and an important part of our walk with Christ.

Find a worship facility that is for the most part, pleasing. Forgive the peculiarities of others. The world will always be imperfect. We must use each day as an opportunity to spread Godly wisdom.

As we travel along and sort through situations that the world tosses our way, we need to remind ourselves the most important thing in life is to submit to the teachings of Jesus Christ. Be humble in the Lord's sight. We do this through faith as we hang onto the belief that God is our redeemer. No matter the problem, life sends our way Jesus has made us winners. Regardless, of the aggravations that go on, a child of God should choose to walk in rhythm with the Lord.

Psalms 91:14 "I will say of the LORD, He is my refuge and my fortress: my God; in him will I trust."

CHAPTER SIXTEEN

Scriptures for Times of Need

We all must deal with illness. The scale of our sickness is not a barrier for the Lord. He is the great physician.

Jeremiah 17:14 "Heal me, O LORD, and I shall be healed; save me, and I shall be saved: for thou [art] my praise."

Psalm 6:2 "2Have mercy upon me, O Lord; for I am weak: O Lord, heal me; for my bones are vexed."

Psalm 30:2, 3 "O Lord my God, I cried unto thee, and thou hast healed me. O Lord, thou hast brought up my soul from the grave: thou hast kept me alive, that I should not go down to the pit."

Psalm 34:19 "Many are the afflictions of the righteous: but the LORD delivereth him out of them all."

Jeremiah 33:6 "Behold, I will bring it health and cure, and I will cure them, and will reveal unto them the abundance of peace and truth."

3 John 1:2 "2 Beloved, I wish above all things that thou mayest prosper and be in health, even as thy soul prospereth."

Statistics show that financial difficulties are one of the worst things for a couple to overcome. God will not miraculously pay bills, but with careful spending, a focused prayer life and seeking the Lord's wisdom in all things, He will teach us to budget ourselves to success.

James 1:5 "If any of you lack wisdom, let him ask of God, that giveth to all men liberally, and upbraideth not; and it shall be given him."

Luke 12:27 "Consider the lilies how they grow: they toil not, they spin not; and yet I say unto you, that Solomon in all his glory was not arrayed like one of these."

Philippian 4:19 "But my God shall supply all your need according to his riches in glory by Christ Jesus."

Psalm 46:1, 2, 3 "God is our refuge and strength, a very present help in trouble. Therefore will not we fear, though the earth be removed, and though the mountains be carried into the midst of the sea; Though the waters thereof roar and be troubled, though the mountains shake with the swelling thereof. Selah."

Most of society is social by nature. Even a quiet person flourishes in a caring relationship. God wants us to enjoy a helpful and friendly bond with our spouse, family or brothers and sisters in Christ. If fellowshipping with others has been lacking in life, then seek the Lord for guidance, step out in faith and join a circle of Christ-like friends.

Genesis 28:15 "And, behold, I am with thee, and will keep thee in all places whither thou goest, and will bring thee again into this land; for I will not leave thee, until I have done that which I have spoken to thee of."

Isaiah 41:10 "Fear thou not; for I [am] with thee: be not dismayed; for I [am] thy God: I will strengthen thee; yea, I will help thee; yea, I will uphold thee with the right hand of my righteousness."

Hebrews 13:1, 2, 3 "Let brotherly love continue. Be not forgetful to entertain strangers: for thereby some have entertained angels unawares. Remember them that are in bonds, as bound with them; and them which suffer adversity, as being yourselves also in the body."

John 14:18 "I will not leave you comfortless: I will come to you."

Everyone has seasons, good and bad. Whether this is a season of trials or good tidings families should call on the Lord first. In times of heartache, he is our strength. Thank Him for leading us. In circumstances where fortune has smiled on us he should always be praised.

Mark 10:9 "What therefore God hath joined together, let not man put asunder."

1 Peter 4:8 "And above all things have fervent charity among yourselves: for charity shall cover the multitude of sins."

Ephesians 4:32 "And be ye kind one to another, tenderhearted, forgiving one another, even as God for Christ's sake hath forgiven you."

Jeremiah 29:11 "For I know the thoughts that I think toward you, saith the Lord, thoughts of peace, and not of evil, to give you an expected end."

Things happen fast in this microwave world. Job obligations and other responsibilities can make us feel pushed. Often, stressed too, because we try to fit all of our commitments into our daily schedules as well as be a help to others. There are some wonderful verses, which will improve our outlook. This first couple of verses is an awesome reminder of why we need to be helpful toward each other.

Colossians 3:23-24 "And whatsoever ye do, do it heartily, as to the Lord, and not unto men; knowing that of the Lord ye shall receive the reward of the inheritance: for ye serve the Lord Christ."

Luke 6:38 "Give, and it shall be given unto you; good measure, pressed down, and shaken together, and running over, shall men give into your bosom. For with the same measure that ye mete withal it shall be measured to you again."

Romans 12:13 "Distributing to the necessity of saints; given to hospitality."

Galatians 6:9 "And let us not be weary in well doing: for in due season we shall reap, if we faint not."

Even with our hectic lives, we must remember to carve out some time in the day to study God's word.

Romans 12:12 "Rejoicing in hope; patient in tribulation; continuing instant in prayer."

Having that one on one relationship with Jesus Christ is the door to having the joy to tackle the challenges in each day. One day at a time, sweet Jesus is more than a stanza from a song, it is a motto that we all need to hold on to.

Philippians 4:4 "Rejoice in the Lord always: and again I say, Rejoice."

Psalm 5:11 "But let all those that put their trust in thee rejoice: let them ever shout for joy, because thou defendest them: let them also that love thy name be joyful in thee."

This great poem can help to get our focus on the Lord.

God, give us grace to accept with serenity the things that cannot be changed,

Courage to change the things, which should be changed, and the Wisdom to distinguish the one from the other.

Living one day at a time, Enjoying one moment at a time, Accepting hardship as a pathway to peace,

Taking, as Jesus did, This sinful world as it is, Not as I would have it,

Trusting that You will make all things right, If I surrender to Your will,

So that I may be reasonably happy in this life, and supremely happy with You forever in the next. Amen.

By Reinhold Niebuhr (1892-1971) Complete, Unabridged, Original Version.

About the author:

Mary L. Ball is a multi-published author. She resides in the heart of North Carolina.

When she isn't writing, she enjoys fishing, reading, and singing with her husband at church functions.

Mary's website and blog page: https://marylball.weebly.com